INTRODUCING AM... PARROTS

Of the 332 species of parrots, 27 are commonly known as Amazons. The term Amazon refers to the scientific group they are collectively housed in; the genus *Amazona*. These parrots are distributed widely throughout Central and South America and human voice among all of the parrot species, apart from the African Grey. However, this reputation can be the source of great disappointment to a potential owner if the bird fails to live up to this.

In order for any bird to become

Most Amazons are basically green, with other colors on their head and wings. Pictured here is a pair of Lilac-crowned Amazons, named so for the patch of lilac on the top of the head and extending down to the nape.

the island groups of the Caribbean Sea.

In size, they range from 25-46cm (10-18in), so are a medium-sized bird. Although some are quite colorful, none can be said to compare with the birds of Australia. Most Amazons are basically green, with other colors on their head and wings. Their particular claim to fame is that they are the best mimics of the a good mimic, a number of factors must come together at the same time. Very often they do not and the bird never talks, so becomes neglected by its owner. If a person is obtaining a parrot simply as a potential talking bird, they may end up being disappointed.

On the other hand, if you are looking for an avian extrovert that will make a super companion, then you could not have any better than the Amazon. If you devote much time to one of these birds it will reward you with amusing antics, obvious devotion, and as a consequence, is more likely to become a mimic as a bonus. Amazons are also excellent birds for the person who would like to try and establish breeding them. Like many parrots, these birds are greatly under threat of extinction in their native habitats. This is due to deforestation and the general disturbance to their lifestyle by humans for many reasons, chief among them the desire for personal wealth regardless of what this does to the environment.

THE FAMILY OF PARROTS

Parrots form a quite readily identifiable group of birds by virtue of their beak shape—they are often referred to as hookbills. Of course, birds of prey also have a similar shaped beak, but parrots are always more colorful and have zygodactylous feet. Zygodactylous means that two toes face forwards and two face backwards.

Amazons are excellent birds for those who wish to breed them. Like many parrots, they are greatly under the threat of extinction in their native habitats.

Amazons, like parrots, are quite readily identifiable by virtue of their beak shape and zygodactylous feet.

Amazon parrots are found in a wide range of habitats from rainforests to open savanna. They live in groups that may comprise of just a few individuals, or larger flocks of maybe one hundred or more. All are stocky and possess short tails and powerful beaks. Their diet consists of a wide range of seeds as well as fruit. Fruits are very important to these birds' livelihood, as they come from regions where many fruits are plentiful year 'round. Although a few species perch on the very brink of extinction, hopefully most Amazons will still be with us in the years to come. Simply by ensuring that you know how to care for these birds will help in this direction. It means that you will not so readily need to replace a bird because of its untimely

ABOVE: All Amazons are stocky birds with short, square tails. This is a Green-cheeked Amazon who is native to eastern Mexico. *BELOW:* The appeal of the Amazon over other members of the parrot family has been linked to its exquisite plumage as well as its ability to learn phrases and melodies. This is a Yellow-nape Amazon, *Amazona ochrocephala auropalliata*, very notable for its talking ability.

As the popularity of the Amazon Parrot grows, so too must the awareness of responsible owners. The betterment of the Amazon species relies on caring, inspired treatment of these birds in captivity.

death resulting from improper care—a fate that many parrots have endured.

In the following chapters you will find all the information you will need to provide the perfect home for one of these avian jewels. Such a pet may well live for 50 or more years with you, so its proper care will be well-rewarded by the companionship it will surely give to you.

Amazona ochrocephala oratrix is sometimes called the Double Yellow-headed Amazon and possesses a yellow head and throat.

CAGES AND AVIARIES

Compared to the situation that existed not so many years ago, the range of cages now available for parrots is truly extensive. It is also much easier to build aviaries today than it was years ago. Materials are more readily available at your disposal. The main requirements of either a cage or an aviary are that it be secure, very practical in its design, be spacious, and ideally will be constructed to give maximum longevity of use. Never get carried away by superfluous aspects of a cage. By this I mean that fancy tops or designs that serve no real purposes only represent wasted money that would be better invested in a cage of larger, more simple design. The same applies to aviaries.

The size cage that you choose for an Amazon Parrot must be large enough so that it may spread its wings without touching the sides of the cage.

CAGES

A cage can range from the typical parrot cage to the quite large indoor flight cages where the bird might even be able to use a wing beat to get it from one side to the other. Indoor flights have become very popular in recent years; which is very good. They allow the bird much greater freedom to move around. At the same time you have more space in which to organize perches in an interesting manner. Perhaps surprisingly, some indoor flights are actually less costly than some of the more expensive parrot cages. If you have the space, they are certainly worth looking into. Most come with small wheels included so they can be easily moved from one room to another.

If a regular cage is the choice, then we can look at numerous aspects you should take into consideration when comparing one with another.

Your first thoughts must be with respect to the size of the cage. All too often you will see parrots housed in cages that are clearly far too small for them. Don't let your pet be one of these. A cage can never be too big, so we will look at the way to establish what the minimum size should be. The ratio of body height to total wingspan in Amazons is very similar across all species. As a practical working guide the total wingspan will be the height of the bird plus 45%. Thus, if a given adult of the species is known to be 36cm (14in) then its total wingspan will be approximately 52cm (20in). These two figures can now be used to calculate cage size.

When roosting, your pet will prefer to use the highest of its perches. Its head should be at least 5cm (2in) below the bars of the cage roof. When using its lowest perch there should be at least 7.5cm (3in) between the tip of its tail and the cage floor. There will normally be about 10cm (4in) in height difference between the higher and lower perches. A 36cm (14in) Amazon will thus need a cage height of:

5cm + 36cm + 7.5cm + 10cm = 58.5cm (23in)

This works out at approximately 1.6 times its height. This is the

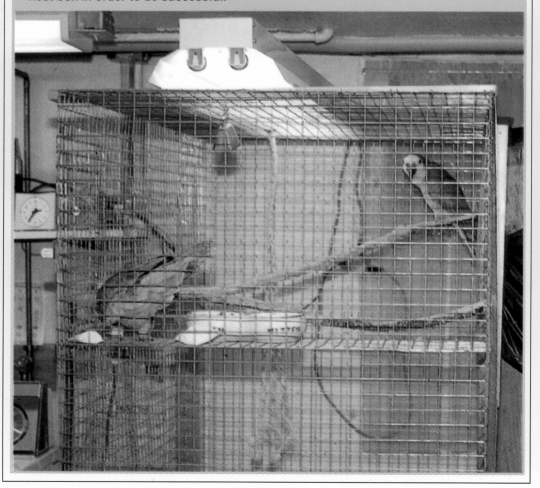

A breeding pair of Amazons will require a roomy flight, adequate lighting, and a large nest box in order to be successful.

Amazons are very social birds, and if you do not have the time to spend with your pet, you should get it another Amazon as a friend.

figure you can use in deciding whether a given cage height is adequate for the species you plan to purchase. With regards to the width of the cage, this should be sufficient enough to allow the bird to open its wings fully and have at least 2.5cm (1in) spare on either wing (assuming it is sitting in the looks, the chromium-plated cages are the best, but they are also the most expensive. Large cages designed for mixed finch collections are unsuitable for these parrots, so be sure the bars are strong and vertical with cross members to give support. Low cost parrot cages will have thinner

The bars of the cage you choose should be spaced close enough together so that your Amazon cannot get its head caught.

middle of the cage). The 36cm (14in) tall bird will have a total wingspan of 52cm (20in), so will need a 57cm(22in) wide cage. The length of the cage should be as long as possible, though typical cages will tend to be square, unless they're of the very latest designs where length is being increased compared to cages of former years.

For maximum wear and good bars and will be less well chromed, subsequently they will tend to rust quicker.

There are two possible door designs that you can choose from. One is a large single door which may open sideways, or from top to bottom, creating a landing platform when open. The other is where the entire side of the cage comes down to form a large platform. In this style there is

Choosing the right accommodation for your Amazon requires time, commitment and study. The habits of these birds in the wild reveal much about their care.

normally a regular door so that you have an option which one you wish to open. These larger doors make cleaning much easier. Be sure that the door fastening is very secure because parrots are really clever at undoing simple latches.

When considering the base of the cage, again you have two basic style options. One is where the cage itself can be lifted from the base for ease of cleaning. The other utilizes a pull out metal or plastic drawer—this normally being the type featured on the larger, more costly cages. The latter may also be fitted with an exterior inclined sleeve all the way around the cage so that feathers and any seed husks that fall from the cage are channeled back into the tray.

Cage bottoms are much improved these days and you can have a cage in which the floor is inclined like a funnel and which has a plastic trash bag fitted so that all the husks and uneaten bits of food fall straight into the bag for easy removal. In each of these style options there is a false weld wire floor that the parrot walks on so that even if the top is lifted, or the drawer removed, the parrot is still retained in the cage. Beware of plastic bases because if your pet can reach any edge of this with its powerful beak it will soon start to demolish it!

Parrot cages are normally supplied with one or two wooden perches. These can be replaced with natural fruit tree branches that are of differing diameters along their length to provide

much better exercise for the bird's feet than a perch of the same diameter along its length. At the same time the bird enjoys stripping the bark and chewing on this, which gives it beneficial fibrous material to aid digestion. Chewing on the wood is also therapeutic for them and helps alleviate stress. Of course, natural branch perches must be replaced quite frequently.

You can purchase uneven diameter wooden perches, or you could shave down the originals so they are uneven. Perch holders for natural branches can be obtained from your pet store. These are better than wedging the branches between the cage bars. Never place one perch over another, or over a food receptacle, otherwise that which is below will become fouled with fecal matter. Always be sure one perch is near a food container and the other is near the water vessel.

Food and water containers are normally supplied with the cage and may be made of metal, crock (earthenware), or plastic. Plastic containers are easily destroyed by Amazon parrots so are best replaced by metal (aluminum or stainless steel) or crock. You can also supply both seed and water via automatic dispensers of a suitable size for these birds. Your pet shop will have a large selection of models.

What you should ensure with seed dispensers is that they will dispense sunflower and other large seeds without clogging the tray they dispense into. The advantage of dispensers is that

Do not clutter your Amazon's cage too much with toys and playthings. Your parrot would much rather have extra room than a toy hanging in its way.

they are less wasteful on seeds, and save you time in filling pots. The disadvantage is that they make you lazy and less attentive of the bird at feeding time. Always tap dispensers on a daily basis to ensure they are releasing seed into their tray. Blow husks from open feeder pots twice daily to ensure there is seed in the pot and not just husks!

From the beginning, you will appreciate that cage choice is very important and that it should be obtained and situated before the bird is purchased. This gives you as much time as you need to find the one exactly suited to your needs. The size and cost of parrot cages is such that any one pet shop cannot hope to stock a very large range. You should shop around and look at the advertisements in parrot magazines which always promote many models. Your local pet shop can then order one for you.

SITUATING THE CAGE

There are a number of very crucial considerations to make when deciding where to place the cage in your home. These are as follows:

1. It should be in your most-used room, so that your pet spends as much time in your company as possible. The family living room is normally the favored choice.
2. The cage should be sited such that your parrot is just below your own eye level when it is perched. This means placing it on a very secure surface if it is not one of the very large models that comes complete with a base on wheels. If the cage is too low, cleaning chores will be more difficult because you will have to bend. Apart from this, birds feel very intimidated if they are not in a reasonably high position relative to you. They can easily become stressed and this could induce illness.
3. Never place a cage opposite a door that could result in cold drafts. This could induce a chill.
4. Never place a cage in front of a window where direct sunlight could overheat the bird. Apart from this, parrots must be able to retreat from sunshine at their total convenience otherwise they can again become stressed very easily.
5. Do not place the cage over a heating unit that is thermostatically controlled to switch off at night. The relatively sudden changes in temperature in the cage can again induce chills. Parrots are very hardy birds capable of withstanding cool temperatures, but they are unable to cope with rapid fluctuations or dampness.
6. Place the cage such that your pet can see everything that is going on in the room. They are very social birds and want to feel a part of what is going on. This will make them more stable in their attitude to you and your family. At the same time, if the cage is near a wall this will provide a sense of security to the parrot.

Your parrot can easily injure itself by sticking his head through the cage bars. To ensure he does not cause harm to himself, do not keep him in a cage with the bar spacing too far apart.

AVIARIES

Amazon parrots are not inexpensive birds and if they are to be housed in outdoor aviaries much thought should be placed into the design and security of the aviary and shelter or birdroom. The subject is vast and if you plan to breed these birds I would strongly urge you to visit a number of breeders to look at their aviary designs. Such breeders are normally only too happy to advise you where they could make improvements if they were to start again. You can also contact your local pet store for design considerations and other suggestions. Building your own aviary is an involved process, and they should be able to provide you with a wealth of information on the subject. Also, be sure to contact local authorities on permits that may be needed.

Your Amazon will enjoy much time away from its cage. Special play gyms can be purchased from your local pet shop, or you can construct one yourself.

CHOOSING AN AMAZON

The choice of an Amazon should reflect consideration of a number of very important points. The fewer of these that are taken into account, the more likely it is that the bird you end up with will not meet your particular needs. Given the potential longevity of these birds, and their cost, you really should not rush the buying process.

DO YOU REALLY NEED AN AMAZON?

The first question you should ask yourself is why you think an Amazon is the parrot you should own. As gorgeous as these birds are, many owners who become disappointed with them could well have been delighted with an alternative parrot species.

Amazons have their advantages and disadvantages. Compared to other types of parrots, Amazons are extremely noisy, very excitable, and are very demanding of your time and attention, but these are virtues to the Amazon enthusiast. Not so much the noisy side of their nature, but what goes with it—the clowning antics, the affection, their larger size, and their undoubted intelligence. If you cannot devote a lot of time to one of these birds, then it really would be a bad choice.

You can only be reasonably sure an Amazon is a good choice if you have reviewed a number of other parrot species—large, small, and those of medium size. Compare the costly birds and those which will not burn a hole

Consider all of an Amazon's characteristics before you bring one home. Remember, these birds require ample time away from their cage and can be quite destructive with their beaks.

in your pocket. This matter then satisfied, you can consider other aspects.

WHERE TO BUY FROM?

The pet shop that carries a range of Amazons is easily your best choice. The advantages of purchasing from a pet shop are that they have experience and can give you good advice, and they can supply the items you will need for your pet. The chances are high that it can sell you a hand tame youngster, or one that is in stock, instead of ordering one from a wholesale supplier. Waiting for such a bird really is worth the time. Give your business to a shop that has very clean premises and keeps its birds and other pets in spacious, hygienic conditions where they are not crowded.

WHICH SPECIES?

If you are purchasing your Amazon as a pet bird, then it is best to obtain a species which is readily bred in captivity. There are many benefits to such a choice:

1. The bird will normally be healthier because it will not have been exposed to parasites and pathogens which could still be present from the wild state.
2. It will be far less likely to be in a stressed state because it will be familiar with captivity—this will be the only life it will have known.
3. It will be totally accustomed to a captive diet. This means it will not be missing any of the foods that it may have been familiar with in its wild state.
4. The age of a juvenile bird will be known to the day, which

The ability to talk and the relative boisterousness of Amazons varies from species to species. This is the Double Yellow-headed Amazon, one of the best talkers.

Domestically bred birds will most likely be hand tame when you purchase them. The Yellow-naped Amazon is one of the more popular species now available on the market.

can never be stated with a wild caught youngster.

5. A domestic baby that has just been weaned will have had far less traumas in its young life than will its wild caught equivalent.

6. Simply by being captive bred means that by purchasing such a bird you are actively helping conserve Amazons in the wild state. In this day and age, when many people are lobbying to ban birdkeeping because they are taken from the wild, you are taking much fire out of their argument.

7. The domestically bred bird will almost certainly be hand tame when you purchase it. This will make for a much faster settling in period.

If you are planning to breed Amazons, then a captive bred bird is still the preferred choice. Imported stock will normally be less costly and may be the only purchase option in some species—though such birds will be less predictable as breeding propositions.

WHICH SEX?

Sexual dimorphism is virtually absent from Amazon parrots. This means that there is no visible difference between the sexes. There is thus no color advantage to owning either sex as there is in many bird species. Males are generally slightly larger than females, but this is taken across hundreds of examples. At the individual level it is not a factor of any importance at all in your decision making process. Males in breeding condition may become rather more assertive than hens. This may show itself in pets with sudden unexpected nips. Overall, in terms of pet suitability, you can thus take either sex and they will be what you make of them. If you plan to breed, then you will need one of each sex anyway.

WHAT AGE?

Without any hesitation at all, I would strongly urge you to seek out a juvenile as a pet. With a youngster you know it has no bad habits, nor will it have any bad vocabulary in whatever form this takes. If it learns to mimic sounds at all, which most will of some sort, you have control over the majority of the ones it will be exposed to. There are two types of youngsters and either will make fine pets. One is a straight-from-the-nest or a hand-reared baby, the other is a juvenile under nine months of age. Much after that latter time it becomes progressively more difficult to assess the age in the vast majority of Amazon species. A young bird will have a gray or brown iris to its eyes. This changes to orange, red or yellow as the bird matures, depending on the species.

The adult plumage colors of some Amazon species will not show themselves until well into the bird's second year, and somewhat longer in some species.

If a bird is displaying full colors in such species, then you know it must be two or more years of age in all probability. A year or more in the life of an Amazon, while not long in its lifespan, is long enough for it to develop bad habits, or to become quite wild if it does not receive a great deal of attention. This is why a baby is best. You may need to order a straight from the nest baby of your desired species well in advance, and such a baby will be more costly than an adult—very much more in some instances. But for a pet the extra fee is worth every cent.

Returning to the tame adult, Amazons do have a tendency to screech as a sign of their general well-being. There is nothing that can be done to prevent this very natural action. They may not do it every day, but then again they might, depending on how they are being cared for—or ignored. Some owners find this out after they have obtained one and quickly get rid of it. Other owners get nipped and become frightened of their pet, so again dispose of it.

All I can suggest when obtaining a tame adult is that you inquire whether you can get a full refund against another bird, assuming retention of good health, if you are not satisfied with the pet as a pet. Ten to fourteen days is normally sufficient for bad habits to manifest themselves.

ASSESSING HEALTH

A reputable pet store will never sell you an unwell parrot, but even so, you must know how to

A bird's good health, or lack there of, will show in its plumage and over-all body stance.

Different Amazon species will cost differently. Those that are in higher demand, the Blue-front and the Yellow-nape, will cost more than some of the other readily available but less popular species.

assess the health of your future pet. A fit specimen is easily recognized, so anything that suggests less than full health can be spotted based on what it should be like.

The eyes should be round and clear with no signs of weeping or being half closed. The cere (the fleshy area above the upper mandible) should have nostril openings on either side. These should not be swollen nor discharging fluid. The mandibles themselves should be neatly aligned, the top one just fitting over the lower. On a young specimen the beak's surface will be quite smooth, but will appear less so on a mature bird. Likewise, the scales of the legs will be smooth on a young bird but less so on an older one. In neither case should they stand out from the leg as this would suggest leg mites.

The anal region should be clean and not stained as a result of diarrhea. The feathers will ideally lay flat to the body surface and will give the appearance of being quite immaculate. The odd feather sticking out or broken is not a problem because this will be replaced at the next molt. Recently imported birds tend to look a little untidy in their plumage, but this too will be corrected at the next molt. The main thing is that the feathers are otherwise in good health. There should be no areas of missing feathers.

The posture of the bird can give you some indication to its state of health. When at rest a bird will sleep with its feathers fluffed up, its head turned towards its back and resting between its wings. It will stand on one leg. If it is confident in its surroundings and you approach, it will open its eyes but may not always move from the resting position.

Compare this with the unwell bird, which will grasp the perch with both feet, feathers ruffled and its head may be in the forward position but carried low to its neck. When approached, it may take no notice of you at all, and will in any case, often have sought the refuge of the area of the perch furthest from the cage door.

A very sickly bird may not even be able to hold onto the perch and may choose to rest in a corner of its cage on the floor. A sick bird will often be seen to twitch its tail in a rhythmic manner. By viewing a number of parrots you will quickly learn to judge which are fit and which are at the least not feeling so good.

LIKELY COSTS

As you might expect, the rarer the species the more costly it will normally be. Colorful birds will normally be somewhat more expensive than a plain green but comparably sized species. Do not put off a bird just because it is not the most colorful species.

A very tame and well mannered Amazon is worth quite a bit especially if it has no bad habits at all. A hand-reared baby will be more costly than an older, untamed bird.

Summarizing the purchasing

process I would highlight three key aspects: be sure you really do appreciate that these birds can be noisy at times—and temperamental; think carefully which species is the one best suited to your needs in respect to its size; be prepared to pay the going cost for a young and very tame individual.

LEFT: Before you bring your new Amazon home, be sure you are ready to handle its temperament and be sure that this is the species that best suits your needs.

BELOW: Remember that Amazons can be quite noisy at times, especially if more than one is kept together.

Amazon parrots prove to be quite playful and will enjoy many different playthings.

Understanding the details of a parrot species' life in the wild is crucial for creating the proper breeding environment for a given pair.

FEEDING

Let me dispel at once an all too common belief with respect to the feeding of any parrot species: *they cannot be given a diet exclusively made up of a few seed varieties and be expected to attain peak health.* Such a diet would be incomplete. Birds of the Neotropics, such as Amazons, live in an environment which is rich in fruits, vegetables, and vegetation throughout the year. They have evolved to survive by utilizing this bountiful array of foods as each comes into season.

The diet of your pet should therefore reflect this wide ranging need, even if you cannot exactly match the actual seeds, fruits and other vegetables that they would ordinarily eat in the wild. A constant supply of fresh water and minerals in the form of grit is also crucial to good health. Grit is essential because birds have no teeth. Having swallowed food items crudely crushed by their mandibles, they rely on having hard fragments of minerals in their gut which pounds the foods into a paste-like constituency. This is then reduced to a soluble state by the action of enzymes, and is then absorbed into the bloodstream.

ASPECTS OF NUTRITION

Before suggesting food items suited to these birds it is worthwhile discussing a few random aspects of nutrition. It is important that you always watch your pet when it eats. By doing so you will not only become aware of which items are favored, but also of your particular bird's general attitude to its food. This can be vitally important in giving you an instant indication of its state of health. Often, the only sign of an impending illness may be the bird's disinterest in its food. By watching your pet eat, you will also become aware of the normal state of its fecal matter: this too is a useful guide to its current state of health.

You will find that Amazons are rather wasteful feeders (as are most parrots). They will pick up an item and nibble a piece, then drop it and move on to another item to check whether it is more appealing. To minimize the waste, it is best to feed fruits and other moist foods in small pieces so they eat these before getting bored with them. Of course, they will tend to consume their favored foods first. If these are plentiful they will do so to the point that less tasty, but equally valuable, items are ignored. With this in mind it is best to ration the favored fruits and vegetables so they are encouraged to eat other offerings and not become picky eaters.

They will throw the less tasty seeds out of their food pot in order to get at the favored seeds. Again, you can reduce wastage by noting the two or three most desired seeds and feeding these in a separate container from other, less readily taken, seeds. This is where a large cage is useful because you have more space in which to arrange an interesting food station containing dishes with seeds, grit and moist foods all in appropriate containers. Do not forget twigs of various fruit and other non-toxic trees as these will be especially enjoyed. Although small seeds, such as panicum millet, may seem inappropriate for a medium to large Amazon, they and others

has a container full of seeds so you don't fill it up. This again favors placing basic diet seeds into separate containers so there is no risk of this happening. Always blow the husks away from seed containers each day so you can see how many seeds are available. It is important that fresh seeds are always available to your parrot. As a treat you can soak some seeds for 24-48 hours (depending on the ambient

Many different pre-made foods are available for your Amazon Parrot from your local pet store. Ask the dealer which one will best suit the species you keep. Photo courtesy of Kaytee.

should not be omitted by you on this account. The fact is that such seeds may be enjoyed by your pet and it will diligently consume these. It will take an Amazon some time to eat a useful quantity, but this is beneficial because feeding is a psychological as well as functional process. In the wild, birds will spend much time on this matter, so these seeds give your pet something to work at.

Your pet may have eaten all the seeds it likes and actually has no seeds left that it will eat, however,

temperature) in a shallow dish of water. Rinse the seeds and then feed. This will soften the husk of the seeds and in this form they are greatly relished. This may be especially so for young birds and those recovering from an illness, or who have "gone off" their food.

By rinsing and then immersing the seeds for a further 24 hour period you can germinate these so they have small shoots. These are also greatly enjoyed by all birds and are very good for breeding hens. During germination the vitamin and general nutritional value of the seeds rises. Do not over-germinate the seeds, as in this form they may not be healthy for your pet.

Always store food in a cool, dark, dry place, and in airtight containers if possible. Be sure the seed is not exposed to rodents. Be very careful when storing oil-rich seeds because if the husks split open, the seed will be toxic if then fed to your parrot. Moist foods, such as fruits, vegetables, and wild plants have a very limited life span once given to the birds. That not consumed over a few hours should be removed and discarded. These food items are best given early in the day, or later, when they will not so readily go off as a result of the midday heat.

The final general feeding comment worthy of mention is that parrots are very much individuals in their eating habits and preferences. Some will like an item ignored by other birds, some will always readily try new foods, while others may refuse new foods once they have established a few items they like. A newly acquired bird may be less willing to experiment than when it has settled down and is eager to try anything it sees you eating!

SEEDS

There are two major seed groups you should be aware of. One is those seeds which are especially rich in carbohydrates, the other is those with high protein and fat (oil) content. The seeds that are high in their protein and fat content are often treated as separate groups, but proteins and fats are invariably found in association with one another. For all practical purposes they can be regarded as a single group.

Carbohydrates are essentially energy-producing seeds and, being the least costly to purchase, are the ones that will provide the daily needs of muscular activity. As a guide, a non-breeding adult will require a mixture containing 60-70% carbohydrate seeds and 30-40% protein seeds. A juvenile Amazon, or a breeding pair, will

All types of birds, including Amazons, relish sprouted seeds. These must be fed to your birds early in the day and removed before they spoil.

require about a 50/50 mix. During the winter months, aviary-kept birds will also need an increase in the protein/fat-rich seeds as these will provide more readily available fats for use as insulation. Fat-rich seeds are actually the richest source of energy, but if not fed with care there is always the risk that your pet could become obese. This will be detrimental to its health.

The popular carbohydrate seeds are canary, millet (either on or off the ear), oats, corn on the cob, maize, and barley.

A wide array of treats is available from your local pet shop for your Amazon. These not only serve as treats for your pet, but prove to be therapeutic because they enjoy breaking off the seeds and gnawing on them as if they were a toy. Photo courtesy of Kaytee.

Protein/fat seeds include sunflower, safflower, pine nuts, pecans, peanuts (unsalted), hemp, niger and maw. Some of these, such as niger, are rather tiny, but may be taken in small amounts. Most nuts, such as walnuts, chestnuts and cashews are protein/fat-rich and will be favored, but are rather expensive.

Sunflower comes in three varieties, striped, white and black. White sunflower usually meets with the approval of most parrots, while black is often ignored altogether. Be sure your sunflower seeds are plump and not skinny. Do not overfeed sunflower seeds. Try to encourage your pet to take a wide-ranging selection. This is easier said than done. You may withhold favored seeds for a few hours and this may prompt some birds to take the selection given, but others will choose to starve rather than be hoodwinked in this way. Soaking unfamiliar seeds may make them more tempting.

You can purchase pre-mixed parrot seeds from your local pet store, but this can prove somewhat wasteful. It is fine initially when you are establishing which seeds are taken, and in what sort of ratio to each other. Thereafter it is usually more economic to purchase the seeds on an individual basis and make up your own mix. Your pet shop dealer will normally be happy to make up the mix for you if you give him or her the desired ratio of one seed to another, and are buying a few pounds of this mix.

Peanuts make up an important part of most parrots' menu, though not as vital a component to the diet as sunflower seeds. Engaged in shelling this peanut is a Blue-fronted Amazon.

FRUITS, VEGETABLES AND WILD PLANTS

You can safely work on the basis that if you can eat a given fruit or vegetable, so can your parrot. All fresh foods are rich in vitamins of one sort or another, which is why a variety is always the favored way to feed. Chop up the mixture as a salad—you can add a few nuts to this and just watch how your pet looks forward to each salad to see what you have included. One of the great attributes of all the Neotropical parrots is the obvious enjoyment they derive from eating and foraging through a mixed bowl of food for real tasty items.

The zygodactylous foot formation assists Amazons in eating. Their feet are often used in much the same way as we use a hand.

Fruits enjoyed include apples, grapes, peaches, apricots, plums, bananas, dates, figs, oranges, cherries and similar items. Numerous berries, such as blackberry, elder and raspberry are also well liked on an individual level by parrots. Most can be given fresh, dried, or canned (as available), and each form makes a change. Some will be readily taken in one form, but less so in another. Likewise, some are rather messy and can stain plumage. This is why regular spraying and/or bathing is essential for these birds so their feathers can be kept in an immaculate state.

Useful vegetables include celery, beetroot, spinach, peas, mung beans, carrots, boiled potatoes, tomatoes and the stalks of brassicas, such as cauliflower. Again these can be offered raw or cooked, but bear in mind that cooking any vitamin-rich food does destroy much of the vitamin content. It is best to supply them in the raw state after they have been rinsed (to remove possible crop spraying residual chemicals). This is very important when offering wild plants.

Of the wild plants, chickweed is usually well received, but there are many others that may be taken. These include dandelion, most wild grasses, plantain, and the flowering heads of numerous garden flowers. However, if you are unsure of the toxic state of a wild plant do not give it to your pet. Again, any herb you can eat is safe for your pet—which does not necessarily mean it will be eaten!

OTHER FOOD ITEMS

There are many food items that, while not natural foods for parrots, are nonetheless taken readily and can be very beneficial because they contain some useful ingredients. These are the foods that are in most household

Dried fruits will prove to be a favored "extra" in your Amazon's diet. Feed this and all supplemental food items in addition to a basic seed diet.

kitchens. Most breakfast cereals fall into this group, as does lightly baked or toasted bread (wholemeal is the more beneficial). Dog biscuits and chow are two other foods that can be given in small quantities. Boiled egg, bread soaked in milk or with a dash of honey, are further items which have benefit. Even a small hard beef bone with some bits of meat still on it will be enjoyed by some birds, but not all. Beef extracts can be placed on lightly buttered and baked bread.

Cookies and cakes may be enjoyed, but if so they should be rationed as treats. Do not feed chocolate to your pet as this can be dangerous. Needless to say candies have no benefit to these birds even if they will readily take them. One Amazon I knew flipped for ice cubes, either of water or containing pure fruit juices. The point to bear in mind with household scraps is that they add variety and spice to the menu, but must of course be given in moderation as treats, not as a daily part of the menu. Crushed egg, cuttlefish or oyster shells are useful additives that will compliment grit.

VITAMIN SUPPLEMENTS

There are many excellent vitamin supplements now marketed especially for birds. However, if your pet is taking a very varied seed and fresh food diet, these should not be needed. Indeed, an excess of some vitamins can be dangerous to your parrot. Only supply them under veterinary recommendation if you are concerned that your Amazon is not as yet accepting a balanced diet.

TRAINING THE PET AMAZON

The amount of enjoyment a family will receive from owning an Amazon parrot depends on just how well it is trained. This in turn will reflect the way the bird will ultimately live the rest of its life, either in isolation of the family, or jointly.

2. The way an Amazon is cared for and is handled by its owner has a great deal to do with the personality of the bird. Sadly, many people have no idea how to care for any intelligent pet. The result is that no matter how good the youngster was

Never attempt to pick up an unfamiliar Amazon. If aggressive, these birds can take quite a bite!

1. The age of the Amazon when it is obtained is an important aspect to consider. An older bird purchased because it was a lot cheaper than a domestically bred baby will never make a suitable pet. In the right hands it may tame down quite a bit (depending on its age), but it will never be as confiding as a hand-reared baby. An older bird that has had a previous owner becomes pot luck whether, with much loving care, it can be resocialized into being a very confident and friendly pet.

when they obtained it, it becomes ruined from mishandling. This point becomes obvious when you see aggressive and pathetic parrots being forced to live out their lives in an undersized cage from which they are never allowed out because they are so aggressive. No juvenile Amazon is ever born nasty or ill-mannered—it becomes that way due to its owner's inability to attend to its needs and give it affection.

If you can then provide the love and patience needed to train the

Amazons can be startled very easily. It is therefore important that you keep your hand where your bird can see it at all times. Never try to pet your Amazon from the back of the head, but rather begin from the front.

they may mimic a sound that you do not especially enjoy—such as a crying baby, a barking dog, or a person shouting the name of family members.

These parrots have powerful beaks and a hard nip from one can be very painful. Young children especially are at risk of receiving such nips if they attempt to excitedly handle an Amazon. Even a very tame pet can get over excited and nip a little too hard when it is climbing up and down its owner. Remember, all parrots use their beak rather like a third leg. They "test" for rigidity on any surface where they are going to place their feet. If it is secure, they will then use it as a support while one foot is brought onto it, then the other.

Once your Amazon is tame, he will sit comfortably on your hand and will not attempt to climb off.

bird you will be rewarded with a pet that will probably mean more to you than some members of your own family!

LIVING WITH AN AMAZON

Amazon parrots are extremely intelligent birds and this means they can be very inquisitive. In turn, this can result in their getting into mischief. Allowed out of their cage on a regular basis, as they must be, they will investigate shelves, tables and other items of furniture. In the process they may knock ornaments over, and nibble on things you might prefer they did not.

If a door is open, they may walk, flutter or fly (depending on the state of their wings) into other rooms. Periodically, they may give out a screech of well-being, or

Your flesh "gives" when the pet tests, it so it is quite natural that it will use a little more pressure to find out if it is solid enough to stand on. Once this is established the bird will thereafter use less and less pressure. If you think about this you are probably no different when climbing a ladder or similar obstacle. If you are aware that your parrot is not intending to hurt you there is no problem, but many owners get family member. They will not automatically like each person to the same degree. This sometimes annoys family members who may get jealous of the pet and tease it. This only makes their position with the parrot all the worse.

Most problems discussed can be overcome if they are understood in the first place, and if a young Amazon is obtained. Your pet will always get into some sort of mischief, but this is surely

An outdoor perch will be well liked by your Amazon. Be sure the weather is not too cold nor drafty so that your parrot does not become ill.

frightened during this learning process and stop handling the bird. This becomes the first stage in restricting its freedom.

Only training coupled with much attention will make it into a family companion. The final comment on living with an Amazon is that these birds, just like people, will give back in ratio to what they receive from each part of their great appeal; it makes each one a character rather than a bland pet devoid of its own unique personality.

If you have obtained a young, hand-tame Amazon, it should settle in its new cage within hours; if not it may take a few days before it feels secure. Assuming you did purchase a youngster, you can open its cage

Hand-tame Amazons truly are affectionate pets. They are very intelligent birds that love to be cuddled and loved by their owners.

door and allow it to clamber onto the landing platform once it seems at ease with your presence near its cage. Once it is on the platform place your hand, with index finger foremost, above its legs and under its chest. Talk softly to it at all times and do not attempt this first handling while there are other distractions or things that might startle it. Early evening is a good time, because by then your pet will be less active than during the day.

The best place to train a new Amazon is in a corner of a room where it cannot get away from you. A bird trained here will have no distractions or hiding places it can run to for cover.

Once your pet has alighted onto your finger you can slowly walk around the room—but it is best to sit down and let the bird see its new environment from the new position of outside its cage. It will probably start to clamber up your arm and onto your shoulder because birds instinctively feel more secure in a higher position. Once there, offer it one or two peanuts or a similar treat. All the while, your object is to create a bond of trust with the parrot. You cannot put a time limit on how long this will take. The more time you spend with your pet, the quicker the bonding will be achieved.

If you have purchased an exercise frame which also has a food station incorporated into it, so much the better. The more time your pet can spend out of its cage, the more it will regard the cage as a sleeping area rather than a prison. It should come to feel that the safest places it can perch are in its cage, on its exercise frame, and on your person. After a few sessions you should be able to perch the pet on your finger and then place the index finger of your other hand in front of its chest so it steps onto this. Always bear in mind that parrots will only step upwards, so your finger must be positioned such that this can always be affected.

When you are confident in handling your parrot, you can very slowly move your finger towards its neck and gently scratch the back of this. Parrots always like this because it is one area they cannot easily reach themselves, but they must feel very secure with you before they will allow this to happen. When you can do this you are making real progress.

With a youngster you can quickly reach the stage where your pet will allow you to stroke its back and feathers—another sign that it has total trust in you.

From this stage you can lift it up bodily by placing both hands around its back from above. Be advised that this is very advanced bonding and the average owner may never reach this level of trust with their pet unless they really have put in much time and affection with it. The odd nip that will occur attempting to reach this state is really justified by the sense of achievement you will obtain. A very tame Amazon will allow you to hold it and turn it on its back on your lap, and tickle its abdomen. Indeed, you can teach it to spin over on your command or signal, such is its trust in you—just as you achieve with a dog.

Once you have obtained your bird's total trust you can discourage it from those excited nips by tapping its beak and saying "No" in a firm voice. It will accept such an action on your part because of its trust in you. The same discipline from someone who it did not trust would be regarded as an act of aggression. It would startle or frighten the pet; its reaction would then be either fear or counter aggression, neither of which will help make it into a friendly bird.

While you must always think very carefully about disciplining a parrot, at the same time you do not want a pet that becomes really naughty and ends up being banished to its cage. There is no need for this with such an intelligent bird. Sometimes, when a very friendly pet gets too excited, it can be placed back in its cage for a while to quiet down.

Do not give in to its tantrums and squawking at such a time, otherwise it will know that if it acts up enough you will let it back out! Placing a cover over its cage for awhile will normally quiet it down, after which it can be let out again. Regard it as you would a child and you will not go too far wrong.

Never use gloves in any aspect of hand taming a parrot. Sooner or later you will still want to offer it an ungloved finger and it will still need to test this new material. You can, if you are very nervous of your pet, use a short piece of thick doweling to let it climb onto in order for you to carry it about. But, again, the time will come when you will need to buck up your courage and let it alight onto your finger so that you can complete your bonding with it.

WING CLIPPING

Clipping the flight feathers of parrots has traditionally been the standard method to quickly tame a parrot. Unable to fly, a parrot will more readily alight onto your hand in order to get off the ground, or to a higher vantage point. Clipping reduces the risk that it will fly away should it gain its freedom to the outside world. However, if you purchase a tame youngster then this need is no longer important, so it is not necessary to trim the feathers. Amazons with the power of flight may still prefer to waddle from one place to another in a room if they are confident in their surroundings. They spend much time walking and clambering in the wild so this is not unnatural to them.

If clipping is felt desirable, there are two available options. Either one or both of the wings can be trimmed. Clipped feathers will be replaced the following year. Let your vet or your pet shop show you how to attend to this safely. Avoid the use of leg chains, which are dangerous and cruel on any parrot species.

BATHING

Parrots really enjoy bathing in water and it helps to maintain their feathers in a super shiny state. It is very important for a pet bird that may hardly ever gain the benefits of rain on its feathers. If the bird is unable to bathe, its feathers will become dry, very brittle, and lack full color. Bathing can be achieved in a number of ways:

1. Provide your pet with a large but shallow dish of tepid water. Let it perch on this and very soon it will hop into it and really splash about with great enjoyment. Never place the pet into the water but let it "discover" this itself. Two baths a week should be just fine.

2. When the bird is on its exercise frame, remove the feeder pots and use a fine mist spray. Your pet will open its wings, hang upside down, and generally show its approval. Then it will settle down and give its feathers a really good preening.

3. Place the pet in the shower stall on a stand and set the water on a soft spray at a cool—never hot—setting.

4. In conjunction with 1-3, you can place your pet outside in its cage on a warm day when there is a light shower (but not a downpour) it will really enjoy this. Be sure never to leave your pet in its cage outdoors when it cannot retreat from the rays of the sun. A simple outdoor aviary flight with a sun screen over part of it will be a real treat for your pet on those nice sunny days.

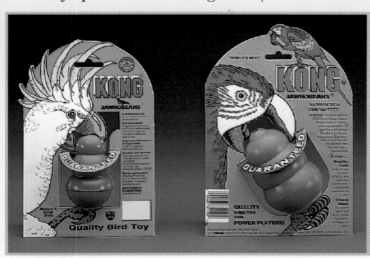

Amazons have very destructive beaks and can destroy many of their playthings. Pet stores now carry many toys that are very difficult for birds to destroy, and therefore can provide your pet with hours of enjoyment. Photo courtesy of the Kong Company.

PLAYTHINGS

Amazons are very intelligent birds and should be provided with as many means of utilizing that intelligence as possible. The simplest amusements are twigs from fruit trees or any other non-toxic tree such as willow. These will keep it busy and provide good fibrous material for digesting. Climbing frames are excellent. There are many models to choose from at your pet shop. Ladders and thick rope with rings

ringing a bell, rolling over, shaking hands and so on. If brought up with other young birds they will normally get on well with these if they are of comparable size. However, be very careful of introducing another medium-sized parrot into your home once an established pet is resident. Amazons, like many other parrots, can become very aggressive to such interlopers whom they see as a threat to their position.

Climbing frames are excellent play areas for Amazons, especially if you have more than one. They provide plenty of exercise for birds as well as a time to socialize.

attached to them and placed within the climbing frame, will amuse them for quite long periods. Mirrors are far too delicate to be given to Amazons. In any case, these are not good toys and can create personality problems in birds.

The best source of amusing your pet is yourself. These birds really thrive on company. You can devise a number of little things for them to do in order to receive a treat, like climbing a ladder and

If you achieve a close relationship with your Amazon, it is very probable that it will then start to mimic your words and other sounds it hears. You can purchase special teaching tapes that are played on cassettes, but I think you are better advised just to let your pet learn from what you say. Once a bird has learned a few words it will then add more at a quite rapid rate in some instances.

AMAZON HEALTH CARE

Being a bird of medium size and stocky build, your Amazon is at an advantage to many of the smaller parrots and birds. Amazons are much hardier than the smaller parrots, and because of this your vet has more of a chance to identify and treat any problems before they become too serious. Even so, you should never take your bird's good health for granted and become casual in aspects of its welfare.

There are many very fine books that have been written on avian diseases and their treatments. If you are interested in this subject, you are advised to invest in one.

However, your efforts are much better channeled into preventative medicine than into attempting to be a home vet. This is fraught with problems and could just cost your bird its life if you are wrong. So, if you are satisfied your pet has any but the most minor of complaints, contact your vet so that time is on your side and not on that of pathogens and parasites.

KEEP IT CLEAN

If anything and everything to do with your pet is kept in a constant state of cleanliness you will dramatically reduce the possibility

There are several methods available to clip your Amazon's wings. Leave it up to your veterinarian or the professional that you have perform this act. They will know which method will best suit your bird.

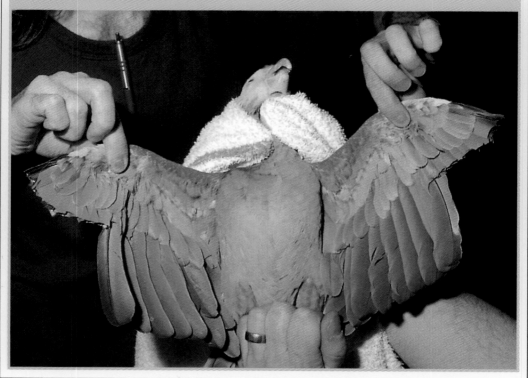

Preening is one way that parrots naturally keep their feathers clean and in good health. Your Amazon will go over each individual feather daily, so do not assume that he has mites; it is his way of staying clean.

of illness. For a bird to become ill, disease/bacteria normally have to multiply to a given level. This they do by surviving and proliferating in the dirt that is around your pet. Then, when the opportunity is available, the bacteria gains entry to your bird and a disease becomes manifest in due course.

Pathogens may gain entry to your bird via the food, via the bird's contact with a surface that is host to the pathogens, or via parasites that inject these directly into your pet's bloodstream. Secondary infection happens when an initial problem, such as a minor cut, is left unattended and provides the site for bacterial or other colonization to take place.

Feather plucking is a bad habit that can sometimes be stopped by a collar-type device placed on the bird's neck. This does not always end the habit, but will give feathers a chance to regrow without immediately being pulled out.

Starting with the food, this must always be stored in a dry, cool place that is free of vermin. Food and water pots are best cleaned daily (at least every other day). Cracked containers should be disposed of. Perches are a constant source of dirt, and as your pet will rub its beak on these they must be cleaned on a regular basis and replaced when needed. Your pet will also rub its beak on the cage bars, so these must be kept clean as well. Moist foods should never be left in the cage for more than twelve hours, and the cage floor should be thoroughly cleaned each week.

Do not forget that you represent a means of direct contact for pathogens to reach your pet. If you frequent places where there are numerous parrots, or other birds and pets, always wash your hands before you attend to the needs of your pet.

Your pet should be routinely examined each week for any signs of parasites. These will be evident on the legs, and around the beak. On the legs they burrow under the scales which stand out from the body as a result. On the facial area their presence is seen in the form of crusty flaking and pitting. Mites, unlike lice, do not spend their life on the host, but venture out at night to suck the bird's blood, then retreat to some nook or crevice of the cage.

Young birds, such as this Double Yellow-headed Amazon, do not show the brilliancy of coloration or sheen that adult birds do. Their plumage is much duller and does not attain full coloration until approximately one year of age.

Mites can be a real problem with breeding birds, because they invade the nest box and can cause havoc by distressing the hen, as well as severely depleting chicks of energy and substance. Again, regular cleaning of cages in the case of a pet, and seasonal cleaning of nest boxes with breeding stock, should prevent infestation by these parasites. Should they be evident they are easily eradicated by modern powders available from your pet store or veterinarian. Repeat treatments will be needed to kill unhatched eggs after the first treatment. It is advisable to routinely treat a newly acquired bird for lice and mites.

BEAK AND CLAWS

Occasionally, a bird can damage its beak or a claw as a result of fighting, or simply getting these caught on a piece of cage bar or something similar. Minor damage to a beak will not be a problem, but should a more serious injury occur you are advised to have your vet examine and treat the break or tear. Minor leg or claw cuts will normally heal rapidly, but it would be prudent to clean these and apply an antiseptic lotion to them.The loss of a toe will not cause any undue problems to a bird, but the source of that loss should be traced. Your vet can attend to the wound.

Overlong claws should be trimmed carefully—if in doubt about how much to nip off, let your vet or your pet shop dealer show you. There is a blood vessel in the claw which you must not cut. Overgrown beaks must also be trimmed. When trimming is needed, this usually indicates that you are not providing sufficient hard things for the bird to gnaw on, or have perches of an incorrect size if the problem is with claws.

The natural parrot beak is hooked and rarely does one come along that requires being clipped. Be sure to supply your Amazon with plenty of chew toys so that he may naturally keep this worn down.

MOLTING

Each year your pet will molt its feathers. This is a stressful time for the bird, and the quicker the process is completed the better. You can help by ensuring that your pet is receiving regular sprays or baths. Sometimes, under artificial heating conditions, birds go through a series of soft molts rather than one annual molt. If the bird is otherwise in fine condition, this rarely presents a problem. It is beneficial to ensure that your pet receives adequate supplies of vegetables during the molt—carrots are especially beneficial because they are one of the precursors of color pigmentation. Color can only enter the feather while it is being formed and has a blood vessel in it. For the best color in the plumage, it is therefore essential that your pet is receiving a varied diet prior to and during the molting period.

FEATHER PLUCKING

Nothing is more unsightly than a parrot that has areas of its body denuded of feathers that have been plucked out by the bird. There are numerous reasons why parrots do this. If their diet is inadequate in certain vitamins or minerals, this may cause irritation to the skin. Likewise, the presence of lice and mites may cause the bird to preen constantly. Matters can become worse if the bird breaks the skin and draws blood. It is possible that they can get to like the taste of this, and so the condition persists.

The oil gland of all birds is located at the base of the back, near the rump. You will often see your Amazon using this gland to supply his feathers with oil to keep them looking shiny.

But, in a well fed-bird, the usual reason a parrot starts to pluck feathers is either boredom or stress, usually a combination of both. The more a bird has available to it in the form of exercise platforms, twigs, and other amusements, the less likely it will become bored. The more time you spend with it, the chances are it will never be bored. Left alone for long periods in a cage it will definitely be bored and will show itself in aggression to its owner, or feather plucking. In fact, if you cannot spend quite a lot of time with an Amazon, then it really would be unfair to own one as a pet.

To overcome this undesirable habit, you must rectify the cause, which can only be ascertained by considering all possibilities and changing them. If such changes are not within your capacity, it may be kinder to sell the bird to someone else who does not have your problem. For example, if you have a number of children, or if you are away at work most days and are leaving the bird alone for long periods, you can hardly change these situations. Another owner, or a breeder with a spare aviary or a need for your species, may find the bird quickly ceases feather plucking.

PROMPT ACTION

The physical signs of an unhealthy bird have been discussed earlier. After you realize that your pet has definite symptoms and is unwell, you need to know what action to take. The first and most important thing to know is that action of some sort is a must. The longer you delay the matter, the more time the problem has to increase its severity, thus making treatment more prolonged, difficult, and costly.

If the signs are minor, but sufficient to concern you, the first action is to place the bird's cage in a warmer location, preferably where a temperature of 30-32°C (86-90°F) can be maintained.

The best heat source is a ceramic, or other dull emitter, infrared lamp. This provides heat without light, which is always preferable. Continual intense light can stress your pet. If the heat lamp is wired into a thermostat, so much the better—if not you must suspend it at a suitable height to ensure it never becomes too hot in the cage. If the cage is long, place the heater at one end so that the bird can move to whatever warmth level it finds most comfortable. You may need to rearrange perches to facilitate this. Excess heat can badly stress your bird, which is counterproductive to your needs. If a heat lamp is not available, a regular light bulb will do. Try to rig up a shade around this so the light is not too intense on one side of the cage. Next, call your vet and explain your concerns. After heat treatment is completed, it is important to acclimatize your pet slowly back to its normal living tempeature, in order to avoid a relapse.

TREATMENTS

There is a wide range of treatments now available for parrots depending on the nature of the problem, and of the bird. Modern drugs have advanced considerably in recent years. These can be administered in the drinking water, orally, or via injections. Surgical techniques can also be used on Amazons because they are large enough to cope with anesthetics and the trauma of operations, the more so if they are pet birds and thus very familiar with being handled.

Should one of your Amazons become ill it is important that you remove the sick bird and monitor all other stock before an epidemic breaks out.

THE DANGER OF MEDICINES

There is a potential danger of medicines if they are not used correctly, especially antibiotics. Very few medicines are selective in the type of bacteria they kill. This means they will as readily destroy beneficial bacteria that is essential to the bird's well-being as they will destroy those that create disease.

The dosage of medicines may be very critical and can be dangerous if exceeded. Likewise, using two relatively safe treatments at the same time can also be harmful. You may be doubling up on one or more ingredients that are common to both medicines, which will then become dangerous. These realities should convince you that if your Amazon is ill, your vet should be the only person who prescribes a treatment.

THE AMAZON SPECIES

Before describing the Amazon species it will be useful if you have a basic understanding of what a species actually is, and how the system of scientific naming is effected in order that every living organism can be referred to quickly, and without any confusion as to which animal is being discussed. This just could be very important to you when it comes to purchasing your Amazon.

A species is any group of animals that, in their wild habitat, will freely interbreed and produce offspring that will ultimately resemble themselves, or their gender if there is a visual difference in the sexes. When, for reasons of some physical barrier (river, mountain), or other cause of separation, a group of animals lose contact with their own kind, they may, over many, many years, and through mutations that are constantly happening, begin to change in both their appearance and lifestyle. At this point in the formation of new species (speciation), such animals are identified as subspecies.

When the differences between the subspecies of a species become more obvious and constant, they can then be said to have formed a new species, and the process of evolution marches on. Within a species there is always some variation in the appearance of individuals. The line that separates individuals of a species as being just that, and those which can be regarded as a subspecies is a fine one. The same may also be true even of species. You may find one authority regards a given bird as subspecific to another, whereas another expert may feel the two birds are quite distinct species.

SCIENTIFIC NOMENCLATURE

All animal organisms are identified in scientific circles by being given two names that together create a binomial name that is quite unique to that species. These names are in Latin, or a Latinized name if it is of another language. The first name indicates the genus the species is in and always commences with a capital letter. The second name always commences with a lowercase letter and, if it is translated, is an adjective, or a noun treated as an adjective (as when a person's name or a country is featured in the species name). This second part of the binomial is called the trivial or specific name.

A subspecies is identified by the use of a trinomial. This is done by adding a second trivial name to that of the species. At the same time the original form on which the species was based becomes the nominate form or race. Its trivial name is repeated in forming the trinominal. This then indicates it was the form on which the species was based (but note that this does not always imply it is typical of the species because time might show it was actually rather untypical when compared to the other subspecies as they are discovered and identified).

As an example of scientific nomenclature we can look at the Blue-fronted Amazon. This has the scientific name of *Amazona aestiva*, which is the species. As soon as a subspecies was recognized the trinomial was needed. The original form identified is thus named *Amazona aestiva aestiva*, while the subspecies received the name of *Amazona aestiva xanthopteryx*.

The Amazon breeder, especially, should be conversant with scientific names because these overcome any risk of confusion with regard to which species or subspecies is being discussed (as when buying or selling stock).

COMMON NAMES

All Amazons are given common names in the language of any given country. However, because there are no guidelines and regulations which control these names (as there is with scientific names) they can often be confusing and misleading. An animal can be given any number of common names. Only tradition may associate one common name with a given species. For example, the common name Blue-fronted Amazon is "correctly" only applied to *A. aestiva*, but using that alone for species identification could result in confusion. If you saw the Orange-winged Amazon, it may have more blue on the forehead than the Blue-fronted. Further, the Orange-winged is often advertised as being the Blue-fronted. Because of the possibility for confusion between common names, you should make sure that the bird you want to purchase is the exact species that you desire.

If an Amazon is labeled as a given species in a pet shop do not assume this is correct. The pet shop may not be aware of what species they have. They are not always experts on this subject. They may label the bird based on what it was sold to them and it may be named incorrectly. You should be aware of the full description of your favored species (and of its juvenile plumage) so you can check for yourself that it is, or isn't, what it is being sold as.

THE SPECIES

All twenty-seven Amazon species are described in the following text. However, less than half of these are readily available to you to choose from as pets. The scientific name is followed by the person who first described the species and the date this was published. Parenthesis around the author indicate that they placed it in a different genus. The common names are cited, the first of these being the one most generally used. In all instances the sexes are similar except, possibly, in *A. albifrons* (Spectacled Amazon). The basic plummage color of all species, with the exception of the *A. guildingii* (St. Vincent or Guilding's Amazon), is green.

1. *Amazona collaria* (Linne) 1758; 28cm (11in);Yellow-billed, Jamaican, or Red-throated.
   No. Subspecies: None.
   Distribution: Jamaica.
   Juveniles: A paler version of the adult.
   Comment: Exports from Jamaica are banned, but illegal shipments have provided a nucleus of stock outside of that country. Although many breedings have taken place in captivity, the first being in 1963 (USA), this is not a commonly available species, nor a popular choice as a pet. This, no doubt, is due to its rather bland coloration.
2. *Amazona leucocephala* (Linne) 1758; 28-32cm (11- 12.5in); Cuban or White-fronted.
   No. Subspecies: Five.
   Distribution: Bahamas, Cuba, Cayman Islands.
   Juveniles: Similar to adults but less extensive red and white.
   Comment: This is a very pretty Amazon but not one that is readily available. It was first bred in 1956 (UK), but most success has been achieved in Florida and what was formerly East Germany. Stock from former Soviet countries may start to filter into the Western countries, so the situation with this species is promising.
3. *Amazona ventralis* (Muller) 1776; 29cm (11.5in); Hispaniolan, Salle's, San Dominican, White-headed.
   No. Subspecies: None.
   Distribution: Dominica, Haiti and nearby islands.

Juveniles: Similar to adults.
Comment: Not an especially sought after Amazon due to its bland colors. First bred in 1971 (UK) but much more regularly bred in the USA.
4. *Amazona albifrons* (Sparmann) 1788; 26cm (10.25in); White-fronted, Spectacled.
   No. Subspecies: Three.
   Distribution: Mexico to Costa Rica.
   Sexes: Primary coverts of male are red, but this is not always a reliable guide. Red of lores is less in the female, and she is often smaller, but these too are unreliable guides.
   Comment: The Spectacled has become progressively more popular as a pet over the years. It is one of the less costly species, at least in the the USA. First bred in Japan (1922), its small size makes it a good pet candidate, with nice colors to add to its appeal.
5. *Amazona xantholora* (Gray) 1859; 26cm (10.25in); Yellow-lored.
   No. Subspecies: None.
   Distribution: SE Mexico, Belize and Honduras.
   Juveniles: Blue (but occasionally green) replaces white on the forehead and crown. Lores contain green feathers. Cheeks green with some red feathers.
   Comment: Rather rare, the species was only first bred as recently as 1980 (Switzerland) but, as with most Amazons, should become more readily

available with the passage of time.

6. *Amazona agilis* (Linne) 1758; 25cm (10in); Black-billed, Active, or All Green.
No. Subspecies: None.
Distribution: Jamaica.
Juveniles: No red in wing edge, and generally paler green.
Comment: One of two Amazons native to Jamaica, this species

Juveniles: Similar to adults.
Comment: You are unlikely to ever get the opportunity to purchase this bird, which is arguably the most endangered Neotropical parrot. It still remains to be seen if the present gene pool in Puerto Rico, which is administered by the US Fish and Wildlife Service, is large enough to

A sampling of some of the Amazon species more commonly available. Not only do Amazons vary in size, but they vary in their coloration as well.

is very rare outside of its homelands, First bred in 1978 (USA). Even if the species were to become more readily available (through breeding in captivity) it is doubtful that it would attain any degree of popularity as a pet due to its rather somber coloration. Juveniles similar to adults but with primary coverts green.

7. *Amazona vittata* (Boddaert) 1783; 29cm (11.5in); Puerto Rican, Red-fronted.
No. Subspecies: Two.
Distribution: Puerto Rico.

enable the species to survive.

8. *Amazona tucamana* (Cabanis) 1855; 31cm (12in); Tucaman.
No. Subspecies: None.
Distribution: SE Bolivia to N.Argentina.
Juveniles: Forehead is green flecked with red or orange.
Comments: Once quite scarce, this species is now much more readily available in all forms—meaning hand-reared pets, breeding pairs, and unproven birds of both sexes. First bred in 1981 (USA), it has proved to be an excellent

pet and a reliable breeder once established. Not the most glamorous of Amazons, it makes up in character what it may lack in color.

9. *Amazona pretrei* (Temminck) 1830; 32cm (12.5in); Red-spectacled, Pretre's.
    No. Subspecies: None.

Amazona viridigenalias, Green-cheeked Amazon, displaying the bright red forehead and lores characteristic of the species.

Distribution: S.Brazil, N.Argentina, N.Uruguay.
Juveniles: Less red on head, no red on wing edge.
Comments: Not well known in aviculture, the species has, in the wild state, declined dramatically in recent times. This is largely attributed to deforestation. It is a quietly attractive species, and is certainly in need of being established in breeding aviaries.

10. *Amazona viridigenalis* (Cassin) 1853; 33cm (13in); Green-cheeked, Mexican Red-headed Parrot.
    No. Subspecies: None.
    Distribution: NE Mexico.
    Juveniles: Red of head restricted to forehead or with some scattered red on the crown.
    Comment: Frequently for sale in the USA, but less so in Britain. This is a very colorful-looking bird that achieved a high level of popularity before losing some devotees when it gained a reputation as being too raucous. This is unfortunate because it is hardly more true of the species than of any other Amazon. First bred in 1970 (USA).

11. *Amazona finschi* (Sclater) 1864; 33cm (13in); Lilac-crowned, Finsch's.
    No. Subspecies: Two.
    Distribution: W. Mexico.
    Juveniles: Similar to adults but with brown irises.
    Comment: Like most Mexican species the Lilac-crowned has been imported into the USA in large numbers, but is less frequently seen in Britain. First bred in 1951 (USA) this is an attractive Amazon that is quite well established in aviaries, so should not be unduly difficult to obtain.

12. *Amazona autumnalis* (Linne) 1758; 34cm (13.25in); Red-lored, Yellow-cheeked, Salvin's, Lesson's, Lilacine, or Diademed, according to subspecies.
    No. Subspecies: Four.

Amazona finschi, Lilac-crowned or Finsch's Amazon. This Amazon inhabits western Mexico, with a range from Durango and Sinaloa southward to Oaxaca. The varied terrain and vegetation of this region afford this parrot a relatively safe harbor.

A pair of Red-lored Amazons, *Amazona autumnalis*, displaying affection for one another. Some fanciers consider the yellow, red, and blue facial markings of this Amazon to be among the most attractive in the Amazon Parrot world.

Distribution: E.Mexico to Ecuador, Columbia and NW.Brazil.

Juveniles: Less red on forehead. Iris dark brown.

Comment: This is a deservedly popular Amazon much admired as a pet. It is colorful in plumage and character. In *A. a. lilacina* the yellow is much paler, verging light green, and the bill is all black. This is advertised as Lilacini or Lesson's. In *A. a. salvini* the yellow of the cheeks is absent This is sold as Salvin's. The Diademed, *A. a. diadema*, is similar to Salvin's.

13. *Amazona brasiliensis* (Linne) 1758; 36cm (14in); Red-tailed, Brazilian Green.

No. Subspecies: None.

Distribution: SE Brazil.

Juveniles: Undescribed.

Comment: Although not rare in Brazilian aviaries, the species is almost non-existent outside of its native homelands, so is not likely to be a species you will be able to include in your selection list.

14. *Amazona dufresniana* (Shaw); 35cm (13.75in); Blue-cheeked, Dufresne's, Red-crowned.

No. Subspecies: Two.

Distribution: SE Venezuela, Guyana, Surinam, E.Brazil.

Comment: Although this species is not especially rare in its homeland countries, where it is often sold cheaply in street markets, it is quite rare outside of its homelands. This is unfortunate and highlights the dilemma of serious breeders. Each year its range

Front view of *Amazona autumnalis* in which the blue coloration of the head is clearly visible.

The Blue-cheeked Amazon, *Amazona dufresniana*, is similarly uncommon, both in the wild and in captivity.

probably diminishes because of deforestation, yet no accommodation is made by its homeland governments for its future by allowing worthwhile numbers to be exported. Though it is true that western parrot keepers have "consumed" many species for many years, it is also true that governments in countries where parrots are native, but are in decline, are themselves now guilty of allowing the "wastage" to continue in their own lands.

First breeding was probably in 1980 (UK). The largest collection of the species outside of its native lands is probably in Florida.

15. *Amazona festiva* (Linne) 1758; 34cm (13in); Festive, Red-

Head study of a Festive Amazon, *Amazona festiva*.

Festive Amazon, *Amazona festiva*. Besides eastern Ecuador and northeastern Peru, the range of this parrot includes a large portion of the Brazilian state of Amazonas.

backed.

No. Subspecies: Two.

Distribution: Venezuela, Guyana, Brazil, Peru, Ecuador.

Juveniles: Less blue on head, and rump is mainly green with scattered red feathers.

Comment: Not a very popular nor readily available species. First bred in 1980 (USA), it was an inexpensive species some years ago but the situation has dramatically changed and no Amazon is cheaply purchased these days. The subspecies *A. f.bodini* (Bodin's) is more attractive, having more red on the head and a more distinct and extensive area of blue-green on the cheeks—but it is also less frequently available.

16. *Amazona xanthops* (Spix) 1824; 27cm (10.5in); Yellow-faced, Yellow-crowned.

No. Subspecies: None.

Distribution: East & Central Brazil.

Juveniles: Less yellow on head, underparts green. Irises brown.

Comment: This is a very rare species indeed, and is in desperate need of being established in avicultural circles where there appears to be no breeding records. Needless to say you will not obtain a pet specimen unless you move to Brazil!

17. *Amazona barbadensis* (Gmelin) 1788; 33cm (13in); Yellow-shouldered.

No. Subspecies: Two, but these are believed to be color morphs of the same species by a number of experts.

Distribution: Coast of Venezuela and offshore islands.

Juveniles: Similar to adults, but head colors more restricted. Irises brown.

Comment: This is not as yet a commonly available species. It was first bred in 1982 (USA & UK) and more successes have been attained since then, so a small nucleus of breeding stock is being established.

18. *Amazona aestiva* (Linne) 1758; 37cm (14.5in); Blue-fronted.

No. Subspecies: Two.

Distribution: E. Brazil, N. & E. Bolivia, Paraguay, N. Argentina.

Juveniles: Head colors much reduced and may be green. Irises dark brown.

Comment: Probably the best known of the Amazons, especially in Europe where its fame as a pet goes back to the last century. The species is renowned for its powers of mimicry. It is a very established breeding bird, with the first being recorded as long ago as the 1880s in France. It is also famed for its longevity and claims of ninety or more years have been made.

They are certainly not the least expensive of the Amazons, which might be thought based on their breeding numbers. Like all Amazons, they can vary widely in their character. Some are very outgoing yet placid, and others can be real broncos, so be sure to obtain a hand-reared baby, or at least a very young bird.

19. *Amazona ochrocephala* (Gmelin) 1788; 30-38cm (12-15in); Yellow-crowned, Yellow-headed, Yellow-fronted, Double Yellow-head, Yellow-naped, Natterer's, Marajo, Tres Marias, Panama, Levaillants.

No. Subspecies: Nine.

Distribution: Southern Mexico to N. Brazil, Colombia, Peru, Venezuela, Guyana, Surinam, and many offshore islands.

To make matters complex, intergrades exist. This means that there are individuals that cannot fairly be placed into one subspecies or another because they exhibit a color pattern that is intermediate between two subspecies. This often happens where there is an extensive distribution range and a gradual change of form from one to another over the range. The following are the subspecies most commonly available.

A. o. ocrocephala. (Yellow-fronted Amazon). Forehead, lores, and crown yellow. The yellow may

Although little is known about the Yellow-faced Amazon's, *Amazona xanthops*, life in the wild, its observed behavior and diet distinguish it from the other 26 species of the genus.

The Yellow-crowned Amazon, *Amazona ochrocephala oratrix*, develops its yellow coloration slowly. Youngsters possess green heads and throats—interspersed yellow feathers slowly spread downward to the neck area.

be sparse or absent on the forehead. Bend of wing is red. Bill dark gray with orange on the basal side of upper mandible.

A. o. auropalliata. (Yellow-naped Amazon). Yellow band across nape. Bend of wing is green. Bill dark gray, paler towards base of upper mandible

A. o. oratrix. (Double Yellow-head). Entire head and throat yellow. Bend of wing pale red with some yellow intermingled. Bill is horn-colored. Three other subspecies, *A. o. belizensis, A. o. tresmariae,* and *A. o. magna* are often advertised as Double Yellowheads.

Juveniles: Colors usually less extensive. Bill entirely gray. Irises dark brown.

Comment: The *ochrocephala* complex of Amazons contains a number of subspecies that are extremely popular as pets, and which are well-established in breeding aviaries, especially in the USA. The Yellow-crowned Amazons have a fine reputation for mimicry. They are to Americans what the Blue-fronted Amazons are to Europeans.

20. *Amazona amazonica.* (Linne) 1766; 32cm (12.5in); Orange-winged, Blue-fronted (erroneously).

No. subspecies: Two.

Distribution: Colombia, N. Bolivia, Central and East Brazil.

Juveniles: Similar to adults, irises dark brown.

Comment: This is a very fine Amazon and has been popular as a pet for many years. Smaller than the Blue-fronted, it is often confused with it and may even be advertised as such with dealers. It is well established in breeding aviaries, so there are plenty of hand-reared babies for sale if you seek these out.

21. *Amazona mercenaria* (Tschudi) 1844; 34cm (13.25in); Mercenary, Scaly-naped, Tschudi's.

No. subspecies: Two.

Distribution: NW Venezuela, Colombia, C. Ecuador, N. Peru, N. Bolivia.

Comment: In spite of its extensive range, this species was unknown to aviculture until 1984, when imported into Florida. It is not a species you will be able to obtain as a pet, if at all.

22. *Amazona farinosa* (Boddaert) 1783; 38cm (15in); Mealy, Blue-crowned, Plain-colored, Green-headed, Costa Rican, Guatemalan, depending on subspecies.

No. subspecies: Five.

Distribution: Southern Mexico South to northern Bolivia and central-eastern Brazil.

A. f. farinosa, Mealy. The crown contains a variable amount of yellow, from a large well-defined patch, to a sprinkling of feathers. Red in edge of wings. Bill horn-colored.

A. f. guatemalae, Blue-crowned, Guatemalan. Head a pale blue becoming slate one the nape. Bill gray.

A. f. virenticeps, Costa Rican, Green-headed, Plain-colored. The crown is green. Rarely any red on edge of wing.

The subspecies *A. f. inornata* and *A. f. chapmani* may or may not carry yellow feathers on the crown.

Comment: The members of this species, though not the most colorful Amazons, are held in high esteem by those who own them as pets. Many are excellent mimics and can hold their own with Blue-fronted and Yellow-headed species. Do not overlook them simply on the grounds of color.

23. *Amazona vinacea* (Kuhl) 1820; 31cm (12.25in); Vinaceous.

No. subspecies: None.

Distribution: SE Brazil, NE Argentina.

Juveniles: Forehead red duller,

The parrot known as the Yellow-naped Amazon is a form of *Amazona ochrocephala*, the Yellow-crowned Amazon, bearing the subspecific name *auropalliata*.

chest red paler and less extensive, bill more horn-colored, irises very dark brown.

Comment: This attractive species will not be readily available to you because it is now classed as very endangered. There are a number of breeding pairs in the USA, as well as in Britain and mainland Europe, but youngsters are few and far between and normally exchange hands without ever being advertised.

24. *Amazona versicolor* (P.L.S. Muller) 1776; 42cm (16.5in); St. Lucia, Versicolor.

No. subspecies: None.

Distribution: The island of St. Lucia in the West Indies.

Comment: Aptly named, the

Amazona farinosa **the Mealy Amazon. Of all the Amazon species, the Mealy has the most widespread occurrence.**

Versicolor is a large, impressive, and unusually-colored Amazon. It is exceedingly rare in aviculture, and will not be seen in your local pet shop.

25. *Amazona arausiaca* (P.L.S. Muller) 1776; 40cm (15.75in); Red-necked, Dominican, Blue-faced.

No. subspecies: None.

Distribution: Dominica.

Comment: This is another exceedingly rare species in captivity, only a few birds being known outside of its homeland.

26. *Amazona guildingii* (Vigors) 1837; 40cm (15.75in); St. Vincent, Guilding's.

No. subspecies: None.

Distribution: Island of St. Vincent in the West Indies.

Juveniles: Duller version of adults. Irises brown.

Comment: This is another very rare Amazon, so it is not a species you should consider. A few pairs exist outside of St. Vincent, where the species is in decline and at the risk of extinction unless dramatic steps are taken to ensure its survival.

27. *Amazona imperialis* Richmond 1899; 46cm (18in); Imperial, Dominican.

No. subspecies: None.

Distribution: Dominica.

Juveniles: More greenish on nape and neck. Irises dark brown.

Comment: This is the largest memeber of the genus *Amazona.* The chances of your ever seeing a living specimen are remote, it is that rare outside of Dominica. As with one or two other large Amazons, the greatest threat to its survival is deforestation and the destruction of its habitat.